Life is a gift from God

Lawson Hanson

Note: Unless otherwise specified, the cited Bible text references are extracts from the KJV (King James Version, circa 1611) with updated, more modern spelling.

Contents

Chapter 1

Grace from God

When God created humanity He endowed each of us with an intelligent brain and the ability to discern between good and bad — right and wrong — the useful versus the detrimental.

God created the capacity for human intelligence.

Although current development work in the field of artificial intelligence is interesting — we must never forget the ultimate creative genius of Almighty God.

Without God we could never exist — let alone think of artificial intelligence.

The human brain processes the information we receive and ingest through our eyes, ears, nose and mouth and the temperature, pressure, humidity and other sensors in every area of our skin and body.

We distinguish between objects like rocks, hills and mountains and the Sun and Moon and stars and we see clouds in the sky and perceive valleys and plains and rivers, lakes, seas, and oceans — to name but a few.

We recognise plants, shrubs and trees; animals, birds, fish and insects and the appearance of friends and foes. We can discern the approach of both fair and inclement weather by what we observe in the sky and feel in the air that drifts or swirls around us.

We can appreciate the rhythms and melody in the music we enjoy and recognise the sound of the voices of those we love and cherish.

We delight in the melodic chirping of different birds and listen to the sounds made by our domesticated pets and other animal and insect species nearby.

We can smell pleasant aromas and fragrances and freshness and also the acrid smoke of fire and the odours of decay.

We can taste sweetness and acidity and sense the smoothness of cream and appreciate the flavours of the ingredients in the foods we enjoy.

We feel degrees of softness and hardness — smoothness, roughness, dryness, dampness and temperature from cold to warm to hot and burning hot — with our hands and even the soles of our feet.

We can comprehend the textures of materials and feel their rigidity and pliability and enjoy other sensations like their cooling and warmth and comfort.

We can detect a gossamer breeze and learn to withstand the onslaught of a gale-force storm — needing to seek shelter at times.

Our brain helps us generate ideas and provides forethought and hindsight and our vision for the future. We have memory for information retention and the ability for instant recall of facts and figures and even visual images about observations and events from the past.

We have learned to form characters and write words and read and speak to communicate our thoughts and ideas and revelations to others.

What a miraculous creation — all on the inside of our
protective bony skull.

Did all these miraculous features of human intelligence
happen by accident?

The result of a chaotic big bang?

I think not.

Why?

Because I have come to know God on a personal level —
through His reliable and miraculous evidence — I'll tell you
more about that soon.

Over a decade ago I experienced an Ischaemic Stroke
episode and discovered first hand how the brain is intimately
connected to the coordination of our limbs.

I was feeling most unwell at work one day. I apologised to my
supervisor and took myself back home by my usual method of
train travel.

When I arrived home I crawled into bed and stayed there
until the next morning. When I tried to get up I found
myself unable to lift my left arm and could not move my left
leg.

All of a sudden the ability to make movements I had made
every day of my life — without thinking — and that I'd
taken for granted — was gone.

Heather, my wife rushed me off to see our G.P. who ordered
me straight off to the nearest hospital.

After a series of medical tests and scans it got determined
there was a blockage in an artery at the base of my brain on
the lower right side of my head.

Brain cells got starved of their necessary flow of oxygen
carrying red blood cells — their vital life support.

This resulted in the death (irreparable damage) of a large clump of those brain cells that help control movement on the left side of the body.

Other side effects of this personal health incident were its immediate impact on my ability to think coherently — in a straight line — and on my sudden lack of clarity of speech.

After much prayer and rehabilitation my recovery has provided its own personal revelations about the wonders of God's creation we call the brain.

The brain does even more than we imagine.

I give praise and thanks to God every day for sparing my life and answering my prayers in time of need and for helping me navigate a way through this rather traumatic event and its ongoing consequences.

My stroke incident came about through my own poor choices over my excessive intake of high carbohydrate foods and over-sweetened beverages — too much coffee and litres of sugar-laden soft-drink every day.

God gave us responsibility over part of His Creation and He gave us the free will to choose our own destiny.

God already provided us with information about the best foods to eat and better ways to live the life He gave:

> 27. *So God created man in his own image, in the image of God created he him; male and female created he them.*
> 28. *And God blessed them, and God said unto them, Be fruitful, and multiply, and replenish the earth, and subdue it: and have dominion over the fish of the sea, and over the fowl of the air, and over every living thing that moveth upon the earth.*
> 29. *And God said, Behold, I have given you every herb bearing seed, which is upon the face of all the*

— Genesis 1:27–29

It appears as if I should have been eating more fresh herbs
and a small quantity of fresh fruit from a wide variety.

I made poor quality choices when it came to my diet and my
general health and well being.

God does not promise to make us immune from our own
stupidity.

In Old Testament days the instructions God gave to Joshua
included advice like the following:

> 8. *This book of the law shall not depart out of thy
> mouth; but thou shalt meditate therein day and
> night, that thou mayest observe to do according
> to all that is written therein: for then thou shalt
> make thy way prosperous, and then thou shalt
> have good success.*
> — Joshua 1:8

I should have been meditating in God's Word — the Bible;
more often; both day and night.

We can choose to dwell in communication with God from
now on and for ever more — or live a shortened life if we
ignore Him and die alone.

At the outset God gave Adam one vital instruction or
commandment — a matter of life and death:

> 15. *And the LORD God took the man, and put
> him into the garden of Eden to dress it and to
> keep it.*

> 16. *And the LORD God commanded the man,*
> *saying, Of every tree of the garden thou mayest*
> *freely eat:*
> 17. *But of the tree of the knowledge of good and*
> *evil, thou shalt not eat of it: for in the day that*
> *thou eatest thereof thou shalt surely die.*
> — Genesis 2:15–17

Before long Adam and Eve disobeyed God's commandment and they got driven out — expelled from their paradise in the garden of Eden.

Ever since that time mankind has fallen further and further away from God's expectation for our potential to help maintain His perfection.

There has been one or two exceptions — for example, we read:

> 5. *And God saw that the wickedness of man was*
> *great in the earth, and that every imagination of*
> *the thoughts of his heart was only evil continually.*
> 6. *And it repented the LORD that he had made*
> *man on the earth, and it grieved him at his heart.*
> 7. *And the LORD said, I will destroy man whom*
> *I have created from the face of the earth; both*
> *man, and beast, and the creeping thing, and the*
> *fowls of the air; for it repenteth me that I have*
> *made them.*
> 8. *But Noah found grace in the eyes of the LORD.*
> — Genesis 6:5–8

I expect you have heard the story about Noah who needed to build a large waterproof vessel — an ark of gopher wood — to withstand 40 days and 40 nights of relentless rains and the ensuing widespread flood.

Look in verse 6 at the words describing the effect our unrighteous behaviour had on God — it *"grieved him at his heart."*

God gets disappointed with us in the majority.

That's deplorable. Surely we must lift our game.

Looking around the world these days — on an international scale and closer to home — it seems we have again fallen below the lowest levels of decent expectation — we miss God's intentions for us by a wide margin.

God created us with great capability to interact with others; we can problem solve and generate new opportunities; we can resolve our differences in a peaceful manner; we can discover more about our gift of life and God's Creation.

Our true capacity goes beyond our first imaginations — it's certain that we can do better.

Yes it will take effort — although not insurmountable.

We need to slow down — smell the roses — and give thanks to God for everything He does.

Our forebears have reached similar conclusions. They knew there was a good and gracious way to live:

> 8. *He hath shewed thee, O man, what is good; and what doth the LORD require of thee, but to do justly, and to love mercy, and to walk humbly with thy God?*
> — Micah 6:8

Here we see three essential points:

1. serve one another with irrefutable justice
   — use wisdom and understanding without aggression
   — no need to outsmart or outwit or cheat everyone

2. love to show true mercy toward all others
   — show kindness and consideration and compassion
   — help preserve life — never destroy life

3. walk in perfect humility before Almighty God
   — meditate in God's Word and talk often with God
   — God created us and has given us life
   — acknowledge God in everything we do

They succeeded for a time and then got weary. They reverted back to their evil ways — like us when we give in to our more carnal nature.

The Bible documents large parts of the history of the nation Israel describing their interactions with God — in whom they believe and tried to please — at other times showing rebellion against those beliefs.

Over the decades and centuries there were good and bad leaders — they had judges and kings and prophets and priests.

There were always people who found the faith to look with more precision at their God and His instruction.

Some of their writers found extraordinary words to help them describe their understanding of God and His ways — helping us to appreciate and comprehend more about the One true God.

Please read the words of this beautiful Psalm describing some of the benefits God promises to us — His forgiveness and healing and the redemption of our life from destruction:

> 1. *Bless the LORD, O my soul: and all that is within me, bless his holy name.*
> 2. *Bless the LORD, O my soul, and forget not all his benefits:*
> 3. *Who forgiveth all thine iniquities; who healeth all thy diseases;*

4. *Who redeemeth thy life from destruction; who crowneth thee with lovingkindness and tender mercies;*
5. *Who satisfieth thy mouth with good things; so that thy youth is renewed like the eagle's.*
6. *The LORD executeth righteousness and judgment for all that are oppressed.*
7. *He made known his ways unto Moses, his acts unto the children of Israel.*
8. *The LORD is merciful and gracious, slow to anger, and plenteous in mercy.*
9. *He will not always chide: neither will he keep his anger for ever.*
10. *He hath not dealt with us after our sins; nor rewarded us according to our iniquities.*
11. *For as the heaven is high above the earth, so great is his mercy toward them that fear him.*
12. *As far as the east is from the west, so far hath he removed our transgressions from us.*
13. *Like as a father pitieth his children, so the LORD pitieth them that fear him.*
14. *For he knoweth our frame; he remembereth that we are dust.*
15. *As for man, his days are as grass: as a flower of the field, so he flourisheth.*
16. *For the wind passeth over it, and it is gone; and the place thereof shall know it no more.*
17. *But the mercy of the LORD is from everlasting to everlasting upon them that fear him, and his righteousness unto children's children;*
18. *To such as keep his covenant, and to those that remember his commandments to do them.*
— Psalms 103:1–18

The Psalmist knew that God is a provider of great benefits by reason of His *"lovingkindness"* and *"tender mercies"* — always satisfying us with good results.

Verse 8 reminds us that God is — *"merciful and gracious, slow to anger, and plenteous in mercy."*

We need to be most thankful for this.

The word translated as *"fear"* — in verses 11, 13 and 17, means we need to have an honest and complete *"respect"* for God.

I love the turn of phrase used in verse 17 — *"the mercy of the LORD is from everlasting to everlasting."*

Think about God. Who is Almighty God?

The Creator of everything we can observe.

We should ask ourselves this question:

> Is it difficult to find great respect for
> the One who has such creative ability?

I hope not.

Among the innumerable statements Jesus made — as recorded for us in the gospels — we find these words:

> 40. *And this is the will of him that sent me, that every one which seeth the Son, and believeth on him, may have everlasting life: and I will raise him up at the last day.*
> — John 6:40

Look at the benefits of aligning our ways with those of God by believing what Jesus has instructed us to do.

Everlasting life in the family and ways and realm of God — versus a short life doing our own thing.

Are we so engrossed in our own affairs we would rather give up the opportunity of a life time?

If the reader has no belief in God — I hope you could get convinced to reconsider — at least give it a try.

What do we have to lose?

At most the hours or days or weeks it could take to read about and put to the test what the Bible has to say.

If we believe man's *"theory of evolution"* — when the real evidence points to God's Creation — please re-examine the Bible truths.

Everywhere we look — up into the night skies and out into the universe — down into the electron microscope and most minute areas of space — uncovering the intricacies of the operation of the human body and other never ending marvels that surround us — we find there's more questions than answers.

What does our rehabilitation and reconciliation to God require?

A set of guidelines, and yes, rules to follow — that we consider essential to the preservation of life — and that get accepted by Almighty God.

It's like the way we have learned to teach our children certain rules and guidelines to help them survive, like:

1. *"Don't touch that — you'll get burned"*

2. *"Look both ways before you cross the road"*

3. *"Treat others as you want them to treat you"*

4. ...

We try to help them live for long enough to learn and make up their own minds one day — and accept the consequences.

We need to grow up and take responsibility.

We need a formula for life with clear guiding principles —
essential laws we will agree to accept and live to uphold with
the best of moral sense and regulation.

The starting guidelines must get simple definitions —
incapable of reinterpretation through any sleight of hand.

They must have no loop holes where the unscrupulous can
wrangle through to another less than perfect and permissive
realisation.

Is this possible?

Is a more perfect way of living a pipe dream?

Is this setting our sights too high — aiming for an impossible
utopia?

If we sit back and fold our hands and do nothing — then I
expect that is the one conclusion we can draw. Did we give
up without trying?

If instead we make a new determination for a better outcome
for everyone — for the rest of time — then there's better
than a slim chance for success.

Do we want to enjoy a real challenge?

Don't leave it to Artificial Intelligence.

Let's use God-given real human intelligence.

We need to wrap our brain around this proposal and figure
out ways we can encourage everybody else we know to get
on-board and follow suit.

Let's make real use of our God-given nous — thinking ability.

If we do nothing then we continue on with armed conflict
across the globe — atrocity and inhumanity inflicted upon
neighbours with whom we do not see eye-to-eye — everything
from road rage to the continuation of wars and rumours of
war.

Humankind can do better — should want to do better — we owe it to ourself to do better.

We have enormous potential — let's use that to maximize the shared benefits instead of amassing more and more mindless detriment.

We do not need to waste obscene sums of money on bigger and more powerful or more horrendous armaments — we need to spend those monumental financial resources trying to restore balance and equity across the world.

We have spent thousands of years — yes, millennia — expressing disagreement with almost everyone.

Isn't it time we figured out the importance of standing in the other person's shoes where possible to help us make positive progress in the art of diplomacy?

Learn to *"listen"* then *"think with consideration"* before we *"speak."*

Repeat the process to reach acceptable agreement.

If the process stalls — figure out what is causing the road blocks. How can these get negotiated?

We will always get sticking points. Is our own demand too onerous; too difficult? Can we compromise in any way?

If not then we need to talk more — not throw bombs at each other.

We need more understanding not outrage.

We need to act with circumspect moderation.

My thesaurus declares that some of the terms that help to define the word *"circumspect"* include these: *"careful," "cautious," "conscientious," "conservative," "considerate," "deliberate," "enlightened," "heedful," "judicious," "mindful," "prudent," "safe," "thorough," "thoughtful"* — with great *"regard"* and with great *"respect."*

I imagine there's a lot more.

These represent the sorts of circumspect consideration we should have in mind when we deal with all other inhabitants of planet Earth.

How do we reach that level of compassion?

I know God can help us make a start.

Chapter 2

Life

We get born — we live — one day we die.

We have no control over where we get born or into what family — if any — we get born.

As we begin to grow as a child we become more aware of our surroundings and our circumstances.

The necessities of life need to be there — air to breathe — water to quench our thirst — food to satisfy our hunger — appropriate clothing for our local climate — shelter in which to live.

Every life is a most precious gift from God.

Without life we do not exist to breathe in the here and now.

We have no right to take the life of anyone else.

We have no right to take any unjust or immoral actions against others.

God's commandments to Moses put it this way:

1. *And God spake all these words, saying,*
2. *I am the LORD thy God, which have brought*

thee out of the land of Egypt, out of the house of bondage.

3. Thou shalt have no other gods before me.

4. Thou shalt not make unto thee any graven image, or any likeness of any thing that is in heaven above, or that is in the earth beneath, or that is in the water under the earth.

5. Thou shalt not bow down thyself to them, nor serve them: for I the LORD thy God am a jealous God, visiting the iniquity of the fathers upon the children unto the third and fourth generation of them that hate me;

6. And shewing mercy unto thousands of them that love me, and keep my commandments.

7. Thou shalt not take the name of the LORD thy God in vain; for the LORD will not hold him guiltless that taketh his name in vain.

8. Remember the sabbath day, to keep it holy.

9. Six days shalt thou labour, and do all thy work:

10. But the seventh day is the sabbath of the LORD thy God: in it thou shalt not do any work, thou, nor thy son, nor thy daughter, thy manservant, nor thy maidservant, nor thy cattle, nor thy stranger that is within thy gates:

11. For in six days the LORD made heaven and earth, the sea, and all that in them is, and rested the seventh day: wherefore the LORD blessed the sabbath day, and hallowed it.

12. Honour thy father and thy mother: that thy days may be long upon the land which the LORD thy God giveth thee.

13. Thou shalt not kill.

14. Thou shalt not commit adultery.

15. Thou shalt not steal.

16. Thou shalt not bear false witness against thy neighbour.

17. Thou shalt not covet thy neighbour's house,

*thou shalt not covet thy neighbour's wife, nor his
manservant, nor his maidservant, nor his ox, nor
his ass, nor any thing that is thy neighbour's.*
— Exodus 20:1–17

Look at verse 6 — God expects us to *"love"* Him and *"keep"* His *"commandments."*

This means we need to ensure we do what He wants us to do.

We do not make graven images or idols or statues of any form and bow down ourselves to those and think that we are doing something God wants.

That is a useless action and God detests it when people do that.

Read verses 3, 4 and 5 again if there's any doubt!

If we take the life of another person — we owe a life.

In our own strength we have no way to restore that life.

Even giving our own life in return for one we take — is an insufficient trade.

What can we do?

There's one solution: *"Thou shalt not kill."*

God knows that is true — that is why He commanded us with words like those in Exodus 20, verse 13.

Each of God's commandments get made for similar reasons.

We cannot undo an act of adultery we commit with another — whether through a willing partner or worse — taken by force.

Think about the content of the commandments in those other verses.

It's impossible to fully undo an act of theft — even if we

restore the stolen goods — there's still the matter of your damaged trustworthiness.

It takes a long time — if ever — to regain anyone's trust in you after that trust gets violated.

What about a life that gets taken by accident?

The courts of law can hear all the evidence and there can be mitigating circumstances — causing them to show leniency.

Did our actions get made without giving any thought to the possibility of doing harm to others?

Could we not have been more considerate before we drove our car at break neck speed through suburban streets?

We have the ability to think about everything we do — before we do it.

We have the ability to be wise and say *"No"* to alcohol and say *"No"* to drugs and say *"No"* to violence.

We need to take responsibility for such lack of regard.

Are we forever doomed?

Here is part of the words God spoke to Moses to get passed on to us:

> 19. *I call heaven and earth to record this day against you, that I have set before you life and death, blessing and cursing: therefore choose life, that both thou and thy seed may live:*
> 20. *That thou mayest love the LORD thy God, and that thou mayest obey his voice, and that thou mayest cleave unto him: for he is thy life, and the length of thy days;*
> — Deuteronomy 30:19–20

Look at the recommendation in verse 19 — *"choose life."*

Our life is dependant upon the way we choose to interact with God.

We need to *"love"* the LORD our God and *"obey"* His voice and cleave unto or cling unto Him — because He is the giver of life.

Grasp the reality of God — settle your faith in Him — and don't let go.

How does God expect us to live and interact with Him and our fellow inhabitants?

Consider this advice delivered through these reported words of Jesus Christ:

> 35. *Then one of them, which was a lawyer, asked him a question, tempting him, and saying,*
> 36. *Master, which is the great commandment in the law?*
> 37. *Jesus said unto him, Thou shalt love the Lord thy God with all thy heart, and with all thy soul, and with all thy mind.*
> 38. *This is the first and great commandment.*
> 39. *And the second is like unto it, Thou shalt love thy neighbour as thyself.*
> 40. *On these two commandments hang all the law and the prophets.*
> — Matthew 22:35–40

Love the Lord your God with all your heart and with all your soul and with all your mind.

That's not when we remember to — or for one day each week. We need to make it a full time commitment — like God has done with His commitment toward us.

God is there for us 24/7 — every moment of every day — listening to and responding to our call.

Love your neighbour as yourself.

Look at verse 40 — if we will adhere to these two commandments — we will fulfill God's requirements.

We do not knowingly harm ourselves and we ought to provide the best of care and concern and comforts for our own families.

We need to learn to control our anger and indifference and extend our ability to show care and concern toward all others.

Jesus also reminded us with these words:

> 25. *And when ye stand praying, forgive, if ye have ought against any: that your Father also which is in heaven may forgive you your trespasses.*
> 26. *But if ye do not forgive, neither will your Father which is in heaven forgive your trespasses.*
> — Mark 11:25–26

In other words — even when we think others have dealt wrongfully with us — we need to find forgiveness in our hearts to prevent us from the continuation of similar poor and inconsiderate behaviour.

The sooner we stop — the sooner we can begin to repair any breakdown of common decency or lack or good regard.

Stop before you open your mouth — consider your own imperfections.

Notice verse 25 says *"when we stand praying"* — NOT *"if we stand praying."*

God expects that we will pray to and communicate with Him on a regular basis — often.

Look at these verses from the book of Romans showing God's perspective on the whole matter:

9. *What then? are we better than they? No, in
no wise: for we have before proved both Jews and
Gentiles, that they are all under sin;*
10. *As it is written, There is none righteous, no,
not one:*
11. *There is none that understandeth, there is
none that seeketh after God.*
12. *They are all gone out of the way, they are
together become unprofitable; there is none that
doeth good, no, not one.*
— Romans 3:9–12

Look at verse 10 — *"There is none righteous, no, not one."*

It does not matter who we are or from whence we come.

Every one of us needs to look to God for salvation.

God knows we fall short of perfection. We will need to ask
His forgiveness when at times we make mistakes.

He expects us to give life our best efforts. Continually falling
short is not good enough — we need to improve.

Staying with a '*dog-eat-dog*' attitude will benefit no one. We
need to upgrade the way we behave if we want others to do
likewise.

How can we show our love to God?

Consider these Bible verses where Matthew reports an
incident in which Jesus took Peter and James and John up
into a mountain:

1. *And after six days Jesus taketh Peter, James,
and John his brother, and bringeth them up into
an high mountain apart,*
2. *And was transfigured before them: and his face
did shine as the sun, and his raiment was white as
the light.*

. . .

5. behold, a bright cloud overshadowed them: and behold a voice out of the cloud, which said, This is my beloved Son, in whom I am well pleased; hear ye him.
— Matthew 17:1–2, 5

Take note of verse 5 and the words God spoke to them and thereby speaks to us — *"hear ye him."*

If God is *"well pleased"* with Jesus — shouldn't we express the same delight in Him and listen to both what God and Jesus have to say?

Jesus gave instruction about how we can love Him:

15. If ye love me, keep my commandments.
16. And I will pray the Father, and he shall give you another Comforter, that he may abide with you for ever;
17. Even the Spirit of truth; whom the world cannot receive, because it seeth him not, neither knoweth him: but ye know him; for he dwelleth with you, and shall be in you.
18. I will not leave you comfortless: I will come to you.
— John 14:15–18

It's simple — *"If ye love me, keep my commandments."*

If we will do this then Jesus promises God will — *"give you another Comforter, that he may abide with you for ever."*

This *"Comforter"* gets called *"the Spirit of truth"* and Jesus promises this miraculous gift from God *"shall be in you."*

Look at the promise in verse 18: — *"I will not leave you comfortless: I will come to you."*

There's more good news. Please read on.

Chapter 3

Second chance at life

God has a grand plan to save us from our selves.

There are conditions — we must want to change for the better.

We must get prepared to follow what God commands and directs us to do — from now to eternity.

There's no promise of a third chance. Take hold of this once in a lifetime opportunity and do not let go.

Do not give in to temptations or wanton desires.

Learn to say *"No"* to what we know is unacceptable — and stick to it.

This doesn't hurt as much as we imagine it might.

We will learn to appreciate the new inner strength.

If we will do what God commands we get given the ability to overcome our human weaknesses.

Look at these glorious words of promise from God — the Creator of All:

6. *Seek ye the LORD while he may be found, call*

ye upon him while he is near:
7. Let the wicked forsake his way, and the
unrighteous man his thoughts: and let him return
unto the LORD, and he will have mercy upon
him; and to our God, for he will abundantly
pardon.
8. For my thoughts are not your thoughts, neither
are your ways my ways, saith the LORD.
9. For as the heavens are higher than the earth,
so are my ways higher than your ways, and my
thoughts than your thoughts.
— Isaiah 55:6–9

God knows full well that in our own strength we will always
fall short of what He expects from us.

Verse 7 tells us God is merciful and He will *"abundantly
pardon"* us — if we will forsake our own ways and our
unrighteous thoughts.

The word *'forsake'* means to stop doing — make the
determination to refrain from and stay away from — all
unrighteous ways.

Consider the words in verses 8 and 9 — these describe how
God's ways and God's thoughts greatly exceed our own.

Take heed. We are talking about Almighty God — the
Creator of the universe — not a mere mortal like ourselves.

We are His Creation — not the other way around — even
though there are those who will try to convince us of the
reverse.

They have no proof of their conjecture.

The God of the Bible has always provided proof.

If you did not know that — please read that sentence again.

Consider this great and wonderful promise:

2. Thus saith the LORD the maker thereof, the LORD that formed it, to establish it; the LORD is his name;

3. Call unto me, and I will answer thee, and shew thee great and mighty things, which thou knowest not.

— Jeremiah 33:2–3

God promises to answer our call. We need to call on God in a circumspect manner.

There's no need to shout. God is not deaf.

God is not far away. God is everywhere.

God is close to us wherever we stand or exist.

If we curse and swear at God then we should expect Him to turn the other way until we get prepared to approach Him in honesty and sincerity.

God is Omnipotent (all powerful); God is Omniscient (all knowing); and God is Omnipresent (in every place at every instant in time).

Please stop to consider the ramifications of these wonderful and miraculous characteristics of Almighty God.

When I first contemplated the gravity and the fullness of the meaning of those three *"Omni-"* terms it inspired me to write a small song you could find here:

`https://www.youtube.com/channel/UCGJLkN1Yynw3g5_wP141S2w`

Look for: *"Remixed: Lord God Almighty"*

My music is terrible — I know.

I hope you may enjoy the lyrics and melody:

Lord God Almighty (Triple O)

Composer: Lawson Hanson, 15–Mar–2002

Lord God Almighty,
The Omnipotent reigns
Lord God Almighty,
God of Love is His name
By His Might He made the Universe
By His Grace He gave His Son
By His Power He holds everything
By His Love He heals everyone

Lord God Almighty,
Omnipresent, everywhere
Lord God Almighty,
Where ever you are, He is there
There is nowhere you can hide from Him
Where ever you are, He is too
When you pray to Him, He's listening
He will surely answer you

Lord God Almighty,
Knows all things, Omniscient
Lord God Almighty,
Knows your thoughts before you think
Though His ways are higher than our ways
And His thoughts than our thoughts
Yet He calls us to commune with Him
To reign with Him for ever more

God is far more loving and gracious and capable than that
for which most of us give Him credit.

God is almighty. God is everywhere. God knows everything.

That's the God whom I know and worship — because He answers my call.

Please keep reading for more of the details Jesus gave us.

When God's Son — Jesus Christ began to talk with people about the ways of God — He gave vital instructions that got recorded for us — such as these:

> 1. *There was a man of the Pharisees, named Nicodemus, a ruler of the Jews:*
> 2. *The same came to Jesus by night, and said unto him, Rabbi, we know that thou art a teacher come from God: for no man can do these miracles that thou doest, except God be with him.*
> 3. *Jesus answered and said unto him, Verily, verily, I say unto thee, Except a man be born again, he cannot see the kingdom of God.*
> 4. *Nicodemus saith unto him, How can a man be born when he is old? can he enter the second time into his mother's womb, and be born?*
> 5. *Jesus answered, Verily, verily, I say unto thee, Except a man be born of water and of the Spirit, he cannot enter into the kingdom of God.*
> 6. *That which is born of the flesh is flesh; and that which is born of the Spirit is spirit.*
> 7. *Marvel not that I said unto thee, Ye must be born again.*
> — John 3:1–7

Look at the imperative nature of the statements Jesus made in verses 3 and 5 and 7.

He declares: *"Ye must be born again."*

This is not an option — it's required.

If we will *"get born again"* — we will gain the ability to *"see"* (or comprehend) *"the kingdom of God."*

If we will *"get born again"* — we will gain the ability to
"enter into the kingdom of God."

If we want to restore our place in God's good grace — Jesus
tells us — we *"must"* get *"born again."*

How can such an event take place?

We're about to find out. First a small detour.

In the next chapter of John we read these two verses:

> 23. *But the hour cometh, and now is, when the*
> *true worshippers shall worship the Father in*
> *spirit and in truth: for the Father seeketh such*
> *to worship him.*
> 24. *God is a Spirit: and they that worship him*
> *must worship him in spirit and in truth.*
> — John 4:23–24

Verse 23 tells us God is seeking for — recognising and taking
notice of people who will worship Him (or communicate with
openness and honesty) in that specified way — both *"in
spirit and in truth."*

What does that mean?

Verse 24 tells us something we might not have guessed —
"God is a Spirit" and our worship of God *"must"* get made
in sincerity and truth — and must get made *"in spirit."*

What does that mean?

The word *"worship"* means our communication with God
when we express our honest and heart felt intentions to
honour and praise His might and His power and His Creative
ability — with genuine talk and discussion.

We need to express thanks that He has seen fit to make a
way of redemption for us — through the sacrifice made by
His Son Jesus Christ.

Another Bible verse explains the *"in spirit"* part:

> 14. *For if I pray in an unknown tongue, my spirit prayeth, but my understanding is unfruitful.*
> — 1 Corinthians 14:14

Here is another conditional statement using the word *"if."*

As a computer programmer I know the meaning of this:

```
if A, then B
```

This states that if condition 'A' is true — then result 'B' will take place.

Conversely if condition 'A' is false — then result 'B' is not happening.

The third clause of that statement — *"but my understanding is unfruitful"* — states that when we *"pray in an unknown tongue"* we will not understand what we say. It's private communication between us and God.

Nobody else gets to listen-in to what we say to God — when we pray in an unknown tongue.

We know what we are thinking about when we *"pray in an unknown tongue"* — it takes no great effort on our part — other than opening our mouth and letting the unknown words flow out.

If we are thinking about a problem we have — I expect the words help to describe that and our expectation for its resolution.

If we are thinking about a blessing God has performed for us — I expect the words help us to give praise and thanks to God for His mercy and His grace.

We'll look at more on this in a moment or two — if you keep reading.

Next we need to find out how we can get to *"pray in an unknown tongue."*

We need to equate the terms *"pray"* and *"worship"* — both forms of sincere personal communication with God.

The disciples of Jesus reported other statements He made to them — such as these to help their understanding:

> *44. And he said unto them, These are the words which I spake unto you, while I was yet with you, that all things must be fulfilled, which were written in the law of Moses, and in the prophets, and in the psalms, concerning me.*
> *45. Then opened he their understanding, that they might understand the scriptures,*
> *46. And said unto them, Thus it is written, and thus it behoved Christ to suffer, and to rise from the dead the third day:*
> *47. And that repentance and remission of sins should be preached in his name among all nations, beginning at Jerusalem.*
> *48. And ye are witnesses of these things.*
> — Luke 24:44–48

Look at verse 47 — it does not matter who we are or where we live — *"repentance and remission of sins should be preached"* — *"among all nations."*

Jesus went on to give them explicit instruction because a great event was about to take place:

> *49. And, behold, I send the promise of my Father upon you: but tarry ye in the city of Jerusalem, until ye be endued with power from on high.*
> *50. And he led them out as far as to Bethany, and he lifted up his hands, and blessed them.*

51. *And it came to pass, while he blessed them, he
was parted from them, and carried up into heaven.*
— Luke 24:49–51

Verse 49 uses the word *"tarry"* — these days we might use
the word *"wait."*

Jesus says they would get *"endued with power from on high"*
when the *"promise of my Father"* comes *"upon you."*

In the book of Acts, the same author, Luke, uses words that
got rendered as these:

1. *The former treatise have I made, O Theophilus,
of all that Jesus began both to do and teach,*
2. *Until the day in which he was taken up,
after that he through the Holy Ghost had given
commandments unto the apostles whom he had
chosen:*
3. *To whom also he shewed himself alive after
his passion by many infallible proofs, being seen
of them forty days, and speaking of the things
pertaining to the kingdom of God:*
4. *And, being assembled together with them,
commanded them that they should not depart from
Jerusalem, but wait for the promise of the Father,
which, saith he, ye have heard of me.*
5. *For John truly baptized with water; but ye shall
be baptized with the Holy Ghost not many days
hence.*
— Acts 1:1–5

Look at verse 3 — after His death and resurrection Jesus was
"seen of them forty days" and He spoke to them of *"things
pertaining to the kingdom of God."*

In verse 4, Jesus instructs (commands) His followers to
"wait" in Jerusalem for what He called: *"the promise of the*

Father" — and in verse 5 He says: *"ye shall be baptized with the Holy Ghost not many days hence."*

The apostles and followers of Jesus were faithful people — they gathered together and they waited in Jerusalem.

The *"promise of the Father"* carries with it *"power from on high"* — direct from God — through a miraculous process called: *"baptism with the Holy Ghost."*

Writing what John the Baptist said about Jesus, all four of the gospels: Mathew, Mark, Luke and John carry verses like this verse from Mark:

> 8. *I indeed have baptized you with water: but he shall baptize you with the Holy Ghost.*
> — Mark 1:8

In the second chapter of Acts we read about what soon took place:

> 1. *And when the day of Pentecost was fully come, they were all with one accord in one place.*
> 2. *And suddenly there came a sound from heaven as of a rushing mighty wind, and it filled all the house where they were sitting.*
> 3. *And there appeared unto them cloven tongues like as of fire, and it sat upon each of them.*
> 4. *And they were all filled with the Holy Ghost, and began to speak with other tongues, as the Spirit gave them utterance.*
> — Acts 2:1–4

Look at verse 4 — they got *"filled with the Holy Ghost"* and *"began to speak with other tongues."*

According to the words we already read in John, chapter 4, verse 24 and the words in 1st Corinthians, chapter 14, verse

14, the followers of Jesus got given a gift from God to enable them to pray to God *"in the spirit."*

This was an audible event that soon drew a crowd. The onlookers asked: *"What does this mean?"*

Peter, an apostle of Jesus spoke to the gathering crowd:

12. And they were all amazed, and were in doubt, saying one to another, What meaneth this?
13. Others mocking said, These men are full of new wine.
14. But Peter, standing up with the eleven, lifted up his voice, and said unto them, Ye men of Judaea, and all ye that dwell at Jerusalem, be this known unto you, and hearken to my words:
15. For these are not drunken, as ye suppose, seeing it is but the third hour of the day.
16. But this is that which was spoken by the prophet Joel;
17. And it shall come to pass in the last days, saith God, I will pour out of my Spirit upon all flesh: and your sons and your daughters shall prophesy, and your young men shall see visions, and your old men shall dream dreams:
18. And on my servants and on my handmaidens I will pour out in those days of my Spirit; and they shall prophesy:
19. And I will shew wonders in heaven above, and signs in the earth beneath; blood, and fire, and vapour of smoke:
20. The sun shall be turned into darkness, and the moon into blood, before the great and notable day of the Lord come:
21. And it shall come to pass, that whosoever shall call on the name of the Lord shall be saved.
— Acts 2:12–21

Look at verses 17 to 21 where Peter makes the connection between this event everyone is witnessing and words already spoken by their well-known prophet named Joel.

While Peter continued to speak somebody in the crowd asked: *"What shall we do?"*

> 37. *Now when they heard this, they were pricked in their heart, and said unto Peter and to the rest of the apostles, Men and brethren, what shall we do?*
> — Acts 2:37

The answer Peter gave is this:

> 38. *Then Peter said unto them, Repent, and be baptized every one of you in the name of Jesus Christ for the remission of sins, and ye shall receive the gift of the Holy Ghost.*
> 39. *For the promise is unto you, and to your children, and to all that are afar off, even as many as the LORD our God shall call.*
> 40. *And with many other words did he testify and exhort, saying, Save yourselves from this untoward generation.*
> 41. *Then they that gladly received his word were baptized: and the same day there were added unto them about three thousand souls.*
> — Acts 2:38–41

Vital instructions to help us find our way back to God.

Not long before speaking these words, Peter and the others had experienced their own *"born again"* event.

Their rebirth came from this gracious gift — the personal in-filling of God's Holy Spirit.

The outward evidence is the audible manifestation of the ability to speak in other tongues — the ability to worship God in the way He wants.

He wants our communication with Him to be free from the lies and less than perfect thoughts we try to express in our own words.

Instead God wants us to make use of His gift — speaking in unknown tongues.

Read again the words from 1st Corinthians, chapter 14 and verse 14:

> *For if I pray in an unknown tongue, my spirit prayeth, but my understanding is unfruitful.*

We could ask why?

Why must we pray *"in an unknown tongue"* where our *"understanding is unfruitful?"*

Please inspect this next verse:

> 2. *For he that speaketh in an unknown tongue speaketh not unto men, but unto God: for no man understandeth him; howbeit in the spirit he speaketh mysteries.*
> — 1 Corinthians 14:2

When we *"speak in an unknown tongue"* — we speak direct *"to God."*

God will understand what we say.

If we stop to think about that for a moment — what God has done is to provide us with our own secure communications channel.

Although we do not understand the words we speak we can be certain that nobody else can listen in on our private prayers and communications to God.

We can pour out our heart to God. He will hear every word. His response to us will carry help for everything we need.

It seems God has thought about and solved the problems of world-class cyber-security long before it ever entered our minds.

There's other miraculous aspects of this gift:

> 3. *Wherefore I give you to understand, that no man speaking by the Spirit of God calleth Jesus accursed: and that no man can say that Jesus is the Lord, but by the Holy Ghost.*
> — 1 Corinthians 12:3

We do not need to get concerned about the words we speak when we speak in other tongues.

We will never speak any wrong against Jesus.

It's impossible for us to say in truth — *"Jesus is the Lord"* — but by (or except through) this manifestation of the Holy Ghost.

We need to receive this *"promise of the Father"* — this gift from God — before we can truly express our thanks and appreciation to Jesus for all that He has done for us.

Jesus gave up His life as the perfect sacrifice to make atonement for our atrocious sins:

> 17. *Therefore doth my Father love me, because I lay down my life, that I might take it again.*
> 18. *No man taketh it from me, but I lay it down of myself. I have power to lay it down, and I have*

power to take it again. This commandment have I received of my Father.
— John 10:17–18

Look at verse 18 — Jesus chose to lay down His life for us.

No man could take it from Him; rather — He made that choice for us — knowing the outcome promised by God — He had the *"power to take it again."*

In John, chapter 3, verse 7, we saw that Jesus says we *"must get born again"* and He tells us in John, chapter 14, verse 15 — *"if ye love me, keep my commandments."*

This is what we must needs do.

On the day of Pentecost when Peter answered the question *"What shall we do?"* — he gave the listeners plain instructions:

> 38. *Then Peter said unto them, Repent, and be baptized every one of you in the name of Jesus Christ for the remission of sins, and ye shall receive the gift of the Holy Ghost.*
> 39. *For the promise is unto you, and to your children, and to all that are afar off, even as many as the LORD our God shall call.*
> — Acts 2:38–39

It's a three step process:

1. Repent

2. Get baptized every one of you in the name of Jesus Christ for the remission of sins

3. Receive the gift of the Holy Ghost

The word that got translated as *"Repent"* — comes from
a Greek word: *"metanoia"* — that means with a change of
thinking.

Get ready to change your thinking about what you thought
you knew about God and His ways — God's ways are higher
than our ways.

Remember what we read in Jeremiah, chapter 33, verse 3:

> *"Call unto me, and I will answer thee, and shew
> thee great and mighty things, which thou knowest
> not."*

When Jesus walked the Earth — baptism was like that
performed by John the baptist:

> 23. *And John also was baptizing in Aenon near to
> Salim, because there was much water there: and
> they came, and were baptized.*
> — John 3:23

We need to get baptized in this way — by a full immersion
in water deep enough to cover over us. A sprinkling of two or
three drops of water is not what baptism requires.

Why?

The book of 1st Peter has this to say:

> 21. *The like figure whereunto even baptism doth
> also now save us (not the putting away of the filth
> of the flesh, but the answer of a good conscience
> toward God,) by the resurrection of Jesus Christ:*
> — 1 Peter 3:21

When we remain obedient to the instruction to get baptized
and do that — it demonstrates our *"answer of a good
conscience toward God."*

When we take these steps then we gain assurance that we will soon receive the in-filling of the baptism of the Holy Spirit.

We need to speak to God and ask Him for the gift He has promised to provide.

Repentance can at times take a while to appreciate.

What if anything do we need to change — in our behaviour — in our attitude — in our belief?

Some people could have little from which they need to repent.

Good for them — they still need this *"born again"* experience.

Others, like the author, could need to — stop drinking alcohol — stop smoking cigarettes — cut out the foul language — make other changes for the better.

What remains — if anything — in our own humanistic thinking that needs to get resolved for the better?

Have we forsaken all our wicked ways and put away our unrighteous thoughts?

If nothing seems to happen for a while — don't stop asking — don't give up on God. He hears our call and Jesus gives us this advice:

> 9. *And I say unto you, Ask, and it shall be given you; seek, and ye shall find; knock, and it shall be opened unto you.*
> 10. *For every one that asketh receiveth; and he that seeketh findeth; and to him that knocketh it shall be opened.*
> 11. *If a son shall ask bread of any of you that is a father, will he give him a stone? or if he ask a fish, will he for a fish give him a serpent?*

12. *Or if he shall ask an egg, will he offer him a scorpion?*

13. *If ye then, being evil, know how to give good gifts unto your children: how much more shall your heavenly Father give the Holy Spirit to them that ask him?*

— Luke 11:9–13

Look at the promise in verse 13 — *"how much more shall your heavenly Father give the Holy Spirit to them that ask him?"*

We need to say: *"Yes please God — I want to receive your gift."*

We need to ask: *"Please God — show me what I need to do to get in right-standing with You."*

You'll know when this experience happens because you will gain the audible ability to speak and pray to God in other unlearned tongues — the sounds coming from your mouth will no longer be those of your native or pre-learned languages.

Those around you will hear that too — there is no uncertainty in this experience.

The experience does not take over your ability to stop and/or start speaking in tongues. You can stop when you want to — you can start again whenever you want to.

It's an activity we should use often — because we get to communicate direct to God.

Chapter 4

What Happened To Me?

For most of my early life (until the age of 25), I chose to more-or-less ignore God — *"Sorry Lord,"* and although there were times when I wondered if God is there, I could find little proof within my narrow field of focus; i.e., self centred on *"Me."*

I guess I wanted God to jump out and show Himself to me, little realising that I would get fried to a crisp if He had.

After leading a rather wayward adolescent life I came to find God, or I should say, He found me; although to be honest, I don't think He ever lost me — I wasn't listening to the call of His wonderful Creation.

Like most of my peers, by the time I reached 25 years of age, I was drinking, swearing, dabbling in drugs, smoking about 30 cigarettes every day, and if I am honest with myself — I was an alcoholic.

At high school one year I had a wonderful religious instruction teacher. She read us stories about the miracles of Jesus as if she thoroughly believed every word — I always enjoyed her Bible readings.

The following year when I got around to asking *"Where are*

the miracles of Jesus today?" — we had another R.I. teacher, a man, and his answer was entirely less than satisfying. I turned away from religion and began doing my own thing.

At the age of 25 years I thought I knew a thing or two and had decided that everything must have come about through some *"Cosmic Accident"* — because that was the best I could imagine.

Soon an amazing series of events unfolded.

Having been out of work for some months I applied to the University of Melbourne for an advertised position as an Electronics Technician in their Physics Department and after attending an interview for the job I learned that I had missed out by one.

That Friday night there was a party at the large house where I was renting a room and I think I smoked some marijuana which must have had some residue of an insecticide or something because I experienced an awful and most unsettling reaction to it.

I became unwell and was feeling sick that night — to the point where I thought I was going to die.

At that time I called out to God saying *"If you are there God, please don't let me die."*; then I fell asleep — aware of nothing until about noon the next day.

On the Monday morning there was a ring at the doorbell. The Postman had arrived with a telegram addressed to me.

The telegram came from the Department of Civil Engineering at the University of Melbourne and they were offering me a position as an Electronics Technician in their department because they had heard of me from the Department of Physics who it seems had recommended me as a possible candidate for their requirements.

I went in for another interview and got offered the position which I accepted with glee.

A week or so after I started to work at their Structures Laboratory, a Ph.D. student returned from semester break to resume his project work, and from this student I began to hear again of the wonderful miracles of Jesus.

Moreover, there was proof to be had of the existence of God and that his God was still performing miracles of healing and provision and was able to provide a great sense of comfort and joy to His faithful people today.

It took about five months before I accepted an invitation to attend a meeting at a Revival Centres Church.

This church has centres scattered across the world. Australia, New Zealand, Papua New Guinea, Fiji, Africa, Italy, England, Poland, Canada and more. You can find out much more at this link:


```
https://www.revivalcentres.org
```


Looking back on it I wish I had not been so slow to respond because the moment that I walked through the doors of the meeting hall I knew I had *"come home."*

My first impression was like that of *"a sea of smiling faces"* and I got introduced to a small number of people who were warm and sincere in their approach to me.

Listening to the Bible talks that day I heard more about the same points the Ph.D. student had been trying to tell me for months.

I needed to repent of my own ways and think more about God's ways. I needed to get baptized by full immersion in water and I could expect God would respond to me by filling me with the gift of the Holy Spirit.

The following Sunday — after having thought all week about

God and His ways I did get baptized in water and I felt wonderful.

There was a knowing within myself that I had, for once, taken a step in the right direction — towards God instead of ever further away from Him as I had been doing in my own strength until then.

In the author's case it took about five weeks after getting baptized in water — followed by getting to church meetings two or three times each week and listening to the informative Bible talks before I then received the *"promise of the Father."*

I was at home alone on the morning of Sunday the 27th July, 1975, praying to God with words of thanks and appreciation and saying *"Hallelujah"* like others in the church encouraged me to do.

I was praying to God and giving thanks to Him for the miracles that had already taken place in my life — in the short space of five weeks.

I got *"filled with the Holy Ghost, and began to speak with other tongues,"* as the Spirit gave me the utterance.

My experience identified in precise terms with the detail of those who received this gift from God on the day of Pentecost almost 2000 years ago.

The experience was peaceful and satisfying and full of assurance.

In an instant of time I knew God is alive and that He cares for me more than I could comprehend.

What miracles had God done for me?

One night I attended a mid-week *"house meeting"* where I heard that: *"God is a healing God,"* and at the end of that meeting I asked for prayer that God would heal my nose which had been in pain for about a year or so from the time when I got punched in the face during a bit of a fight.

The person who prayed for me more-or-less said, *"Thank you God for healing this man's nose."*, and then I went home.

During the night I woke up feeling rather warm, but there was also a tingling sensation in the middle of my face. I got up out of bed to check that there was nobody there — I used to live alone.

In the middle of Winter where I lived, I soon cooled down and then went back to sleep.

In the morning there was another strange sensation: No more pain!

Miraculously that pain got removed overnight.

At another house meeting I remember hearing it said that *"God can do anything"* and I took it upon myself to say to God: *"Okay God. If you can do anything: Stop me from smoking (cigarettes)."* — I think I forgot to say *"Please."* *"Sorry Lord."*

Later that night when I got home I went to light up a cigarette before heading off to bed.

For some reason — that cigarette tasted awful.

I had another new carton of cigarettes in the cupboard. I opened that, took out a fresh pack, and lit up another cigarette and guess what? That one tasted awful, too.

Almost in disgust, I think, I went to bed and slept soundly until the next morning. When I awoke, I again tried to light up another cigarette; and ... you guessed it: that one also tasted disgusting!

Since that day I have never had the craving for another cigarette. The slightest smell of cigarette smoke makes me feel rather ill.

God helped me to stop smoking overnight — and moreover, I experienced no residual cravings from the addictive stimulant effects of nicotine.

Soon the desire to drink alcohol deserted me and one day I had the urge to pour my entire collection of beer and wines and spirits down the sink.

I rounded up all the cans and bottles and lined them up near the sink and then almost ceremoniously — I poured out their entire content — smiling as I did and it felt most liberating.

Since doing that I have never wanted to touch another glass of beer or alcohol of any kind. And another thing, my speech was beginning contain less and less profanities.

I give God the glory for removing my alcohol addiction and for cleaning up my thinking and my speech.

These miracles — plus a realisation that my sense of taste and smell was beginning to return and that I was sleeping soundly every night — instead of tossing and turning half awake for hours on end (as I had been before).

What a wonderful God we have — I praise Him for His abundant grace and mercy.

As I was thinking about those miracles that God had already performed for me, I realized that I had actually received the gift of the Holy Spirit, and was speaking in other tongues in a quiet normal tone of voice.

The words coming from my mouth changed from my native English tongue to those of words in an unknown language I'd never before heard or learned.

Until the day I received the gift of the Holy Ghost, I had often wondered at the answer to the age-old question: *"What is the meaning of life?"*

When that experience happened to me, in a brief moment of

time, everything made sense.

In that instant I knew: God is alive and He cares for and loves His creation and He has a plan of salvation for us and now access to the realm of God is available to anyone who will seek Him and ask of Him.

I once heard a friend put it this way: *"Life is a time when we get to choose if we want to be a part of God's eternity."* Of course we need to believe that God exists, and that He has a wonderful plan with which we want to be a part.

We need to want to know God enough to ask Him to let us have a share in His plan of salvation.

God does not impose Himself upon us — not yet anyway, although a day of reckoning will no doubt come.

God wants to commune with His creation — He wants this to be a two-way street.

If God wanted robots He could make squillions of them; but He doesn't want that.

A *'squillion'* is the indeterminable number of robots God could make if He used all the matter in the known universe and then some — if He chose to do that.

God created men and women with the capacity to love and enjoy their relationship with Him.

He gave us free will so that we could choose to enter into that relationship with Him, or we could choose to opt out.

With the gift of free will comes the awful realisation that some people will not want to do that ... but that is their own free will, i.e., of their own choosing.

If we choose to go it alone, then we might expect to live for seventy years or so, and then to die like everyone else.

If we choose to obey the Word of God, and repent and get

baptised as requested (or instructed, or commanded), then we can expect to live forever.

Certainly, we may die naturally, sooner or later, but the promise of God is that there is more to come. Again, God's Word promises:

> 52. *In a moment, in the twinkling of an eye, at the last trumpet. For the trumpet will sound, and the dead will be raised incorruptible, and we shall be changed.*
> — I Corinthians 15:52 (KJV)

Don't let anybody try to tell you there's no God.

God is alive and powerful and real as ever and He is waiting to answer our call.

God has pre-defined the way in which He will answer us — so we know we have reached and made secure contact with Almighty God — the Creator of the universe — the Creator of All.

None other than Almighty God can answer us in this way.

The grace and mercy of God is miraculous — from everlasting to everlasting.

There's One God:

> 22. *Look unto me, and be ye saved, all the ends of the earth: for I am God, and there is none else.*
> — Isaiah 45:22

By His Spirit that now dwells within us from that moment forward — He leads and guides and provides miracles and great care and comfort to His people.

Since that time — over fifty years ago, I have seen hundreds and know about thousands of other people who have put God's Word to the test and who have gained the same result.

God promises to answer us if we will call upon Him.

God has a wonderful gift available for us to receive.

For almost two thousand years God's gift has been available to everyone, everywhere — *"I will pour out my Spirit upon all flesh."*

God's gift carries with it great assurance and evidence that none other than God can provide.

God's gift leaves us in total control of what we do — open our mouth and speak in unlearned tongues or open our mouth and speak in our native tongue — the choice is ours.

If we ignore God's gift we could get counted among those about whom the Psalmist wrote using these words:

> 1. *The fool hath said in his heart, There is no God. They are corrupt, they have done abominable works, there is none that doeth good.*
> — Psalms 14:1

I recommend asking God — He promises to answer our humble and sincere call — Jeremiah 33:3.

Chapter 5

Holy Spirit Guidance

When we get Spirit filled we should walk in newness of life.

The New Testament books from Acts onwards offer much advice about how we should live and how we can expect to do that with the help of God and our new in-dwelling gift of the Holy Spirit.

In the book of Romans, chapter 12, we read:

> 1. *I beseech you therefore, brethren, by the mercies of God, that ye present your bodies a living sacrifice, holy, acceptable unto God, which is your reasonable service.*
> 2. *And be not conformed to this world: but be ye transformed by the renewing of your mind, that ye may prove what is that good, and acceptable, and perfect, will of God.*
> 3. *For I say, through the grace given unto me, to every man that is among you, not to think of himself more highly than he ought to think; but to think soberly, according as God hath dealt to every man the measure of faith.*
> — Romans 12:1–3

We have no need to conform to the ways of the world. We have a new enlightened dimension — *"transformed by the renewing of your mind"* — in which we can live and breathe and move and enjoy life.

A wonderful part of God's gift to us is described in the last clause of verse 3 with these words:

> *"God hath dealt to every man the measure of faith."*

God shows no partiality when He pours out His Holy Spirit upon those who will hear His call and ask for His gift. We each receive *"the measure of faith"* to help us get through our life here on Earth.

When Jesus told Nicodemus: *"Ye must be born again."* — the terminology He used is most apt.

The refreshing gift of the Holy Spirit gives us the power to turn over a new page and begin to live the kind of life God expects us to enjoy.

Using the gift of praying in unknown tongues we get to communicate with God every moment of every day.

What a privileged position we have inherited — all because Jesus chose to sacrifice His life to take away our sins and pave the way for our salvation.

The little book of Jude contains important information for us to consider and a vital point to appreciate about *"praying in the Holy Ghost"*:

> 17. *But, beloved, remember ye the words which were spoken before of the apostles of our Lord Jesus Christ;*
> 18. *How that they told you there should be mockers in the last time, who should walk after their own ungodly lusts.*

19. *These be they who separate themselves,*
sensual, having not the Spirit.
20. *But ye, beloved, building up yourselves on*
your most holy faith, praying in the Holy Ghost,
21. *Keep yourselves in the love of God, looking for*
the mercy of our Lord Jesus Christ unto eternal
life.
— Jude 1:17–21

We should not get surprised when we find people who will try to make a mockery of our new found faith in God — don't get upset — we got told this could happen.

Why do people do that? Because unlike us — they do not have God's Spirit — they have no personal experience of the power of God in their life — unlike the certainty we have now received.

Verse 20 reminds us that the activity of *"praying in the Holy Ghost"* — praying in our unknown tongue — will help in *"building up yourselves."* It helps to keep us strong in our faith toward God.

Paul, the writer of the book of Romans gives us practical advice about how we ought to conduct ourselves and our affairs:

9. *Let love be without dissimulation. Abhor that*
which is evil; cleave to that which is good.
10. *Be kindly affectioned one to another with*
brotherly love; in honour preferring one another;
11. *Not slothful in business; fervent in spirit;*
serving the Lord;
12. *Rejoicing in hope; patient in tribulation;*
continuing instant in prayer;
13. *Distributing to the necessity of saints; given to*
hospitality.

14. *Bless them which persecute you: bless, and
curse not.*
15. *Rejoice with them that do rejoice, and weep
with them that weep.*
16. *Be of the same mind one toward another.
Mind not high things, but condescend to men of
low estate. Be not wise in your own conceits.*
17. *Recompense to no man evil for evil. Provide
things honest in the sight of all men.*
18. *If it be possible, as much as lieth in you, live
peaceably with all men.*
— Romans 12:9–18

In verse 16, the word "*condescend*" implies no overbearing
superiority — rather, it suggests we come down from our
high horse and mix more freely with those whom we might
have tended to shun before.

Everyone who receives the gift of the Holy Spirit is equal in
the sight of God — and should get treated by us in the same
manner.

Again, Paul, writing to the church at Galatia provides this
sobering advice:

16. *This I say then, Walk in the Spirit, and ye
shall not fulfil the lust of the flesh.*
17. *For the flesh lusteth against the Spirit, and the
Spirit against the flesh: and these are contrary the
one to the other: so that ye cannot do the things
that ye would.*
18. *But if ye be led of the Spirit, ye are not under
the law.*
19. *Now the works of the flesh are manifest, which
are these; Adultery, fornication, uncleanness,
lasciviousness,*
20. *Idolatry, witchcraft, hatred, variance,
emulations, wrath, strife, seditions, heresies,*

*21. Envyings, murders, drunkenness, revellings,
and such like: of the which I tell you before, as I
have also told you in time past, that they which do
such things shall not inherit the kingdom of God.*
— Galatians 5:16–21

We need to change gears so we now *"Walk in the Spirit."*

Stop and think first: *"Is this acceptable to God and His
ways?"*

How do we change from the unrighteous person we were to
the kind of person God wants us to become and remain?

From now on we never entertain the idea of getting involved
in any of those activities listed in verses 19, 20 and 21.

Look at the last clause in verse 21:

> *"they which do such things shall not inherit the
> kingdom of God."*

We need to determine in our mind to stay away from all
those ways of the world and keep ourselves separate from
those who conduct such unrighteous activity — even if
that includes family members and long-time friends or
acquaintances.

Be swift to say *"No"* to any such invitation to get involved
in organised events and wanton partying in which you will no
longer participate.

The first time is often the hardest. After a while people begin
to realise that we have chosen to walk on the straight and
narrow path — be a good testimony to them by remaining
steadfast to the Lord's principles.

God does not leave us to our own devices — rather, He
endows us with a wonderful set of personal characteristics
that Paul calls *"the fruit of the Spirit."*

22. But the fruit of the Spirit is love, joy, peace, longsuffering, gentleness, goodness, faith,
23. Meekness, temperance: against such there is no law.
— Galatians 5:22–23

We have direct personal access to these *"fruit of the Spirit"* in far greater measure than we might have managed before — under our own steam.

This set of nine delightful behavioural characteristics inspired me to write a three line song — perhaps more like a nursery rhyme. The words were already there — all I did is write a simple melody.

It helps me remember those Spiritual Fruit whenever I find myself needing more patience or a better level of self control.

You could find that with its words and melody described in Lilypond notation in another small book titled:

"Love, Joy, Peace"
ISBN: 9791764057844 (EPUB)
ISBN: 9791764057851 (paper book)

I sing this little song (to myself) to remind me that God has given us more of each of these behavioural capabilities to help us stop and re-evaluate any difficult or awkward moments or events — and navigate a better pathway in life.

Through the in-filling of the Holy Spirit — God has given us the wherewithal to rise above the entrapments of the crude and unworthy elements of life.

One of the best commitments we can make is to continue getting to church meetings where we can rub shoulders — have fellowship — with like-minded faithful people who have also received God's gift of the Holy Spirit.

Make this first priority in your life — re-arrange other events to take place at other times — not at times when there's a church meeting to attend.

This is what those who first received this gift from God did:

> 42. *And they continued stedfastly in the apostles'*
> *doctrine and fellowship, and in breaking of bread,*
> *and in prayers.*
> — Acts 2:42

Make it a habit to get to church before the meeting start times and talk to your brothers and sisters in Christ.

This is another time when we will hear more personal testimonies of how people came to The Lord and how they overcame awkward issues in their life or gained a whole range of comfort and provision and healing miracles from God through the action of exercising their faith in prayer.

Make it your aspiration to get something from every Bible talk you hear — parts you've heard before should re-enforce the finer points.

Don't ever get tired of reading through God's Word.

The writer of the book called *"Hebrews"* provides us with this advice:

> 23. *Let us hold fast the profession of our*
> *faith without wavering; (for he is faithful that*
> *promised;)*
> 24. *And let us consider one another to provoke*
> *unto love and to good works:*
> 25. *Not forsaking the assembling of ourselves*
> *together, as the manner of some is; but exhorting*
> *one another: and so much the more, as ye see the*
> *day approaching.*
> — Hebrews 10:23–25

Look at these words in verse 25: *"Not forsaking the assembling of ourselves together."* We need to be there *"exhorting"* — encouraging each other to *"hold fast"* — *"as we see the day"* (of Jesus' Return) *"approaching."*

Let's give God's born again experience every opportunity to flourish in our life — it has the promise of everlasting life.

Luke wrote that Jesus Christ gave His followers this advice:

> 34. *And take heed to yourselves, lest at any time your hearts be overcharged with surfeiting, and drunkenness, and cares of this life, and so that day come upon you unawares.*
> 35. *For as a snare shall it come on all them that dwell on the face of the whole earth.*
> 36. *Watch ye therefore, and pray always, that ye may be accounted worthy to escape all these things that shall come to pass, and to stand before the Son of man.*
> — Luke 21:34–36

From another perspective, writing to the church at Corinth, we get encouraged to *"come out"* and *"be separate"* from those who do not believe the full gospel of Jesus Christ:

> 14. *Be ye not unequally yoked together with unbelievers: for what fellowship hath righteousness with unrighteousness? and what communion hath light with darkness?*
> 15. *And what concord hath Christ with Belial? or what part hath he that believeth with an infidel?*
> 16. *And what agreement hath the temple of God with idols? for ye are the temple of the living God; as God hath said, I will dwell in them, and walk in them; and I will be their God, and they shall be my people.*

> 17. *Wherefore come out from among them, and
> be ye separate, saith the Lord, and touch not the
> unclean thing; and I will receive you.*
> 18. *And will be a Father unto you, and ye shall be
> my sons and daughters, saith the Lord Almighty.*
> — 2 Corinthians 6:14–18

The benefits of following such advice gets described in verse
18 — God *will be a Father unto you and ye shall be my sons
and daughters* — as promised by the Lord Almighty.

We need to make a clean break away from any old church or
religious organisation that does not preach the whole truth of
God. These could be *"Christian"* in name only.

Jesus Christ says we *"must get born again"* — John 3:7.

The book of James has these words to say:

> 22. *But be ye doers of the word, and not hearers
> only, deceiving your own selves.*
> 23. *For if any be a hearer of the word, and not a
> doer, he is like unto a man beholding his natural
> face in a glass:*
> 24. *For he beholdeth himself, and goeth his way,
> and straightway forgetteth what manner of man he
> was.*
> 25. *But whoso looketh into the perfect law of
> liberty, and continueth therein, he being not a
> forgetful hearer, but a doer of the work, this man
> shall be blessed in his deed.*
> — James 1:22–25

The Bible says *"God is a Spirit"* and we *"must worship Him
in spirit and in truth"* — John 4:24.

We must receive God's gift of the baptism in the Holy Ghost
that enables us to speak in unlearned tongues giving us the
ability to fulfill that necessary part of the relationship.

The book of 1st Corinthians and chapters 12, 13 and 14, provide instruction for us about the miraculous gifts of the Spirit that God has now given to us — all who have received His Holy Spirit with its audible ability to let us speak in other unlearned tongues.

These verses from chapter 12 identify these nine different spiritual gifts:

> 7. *But the manifestation of the Spirit is given to every man to profit withal.*
> 8. *For to one is given by the Spirit the word of wisdom; to another the word of knowledge by the same Spirit;*
> 9. *To another faith by the same Spirit; to another the gifts of healing by the same Spirit;*
> 10. *To another the working of miracles; to another prophecy; to another discerning of spirits; to another divers kinds of tongues; to another the interpretation of tongues:*
> 11. *But all these worketh that one and the selfsame Spirit, dividing to every man severally as he will.*
> — 1 Corinthians 12:7–11

On first reading it's easy to imagine those verses say that person A will get gift X and person B will get gift Y while person C gets gift Z and then that is the end of the matter.

When read in context with all the Bible has to say we find verse 7 means what it says:

> *But the manifestation of the Spirit is given to every man to profit withal.*

Although at any one time this person or that person could use the gift of healing or will speak out to interpret a message

another has spoken in tongues — this does not prevent them
— or any other Spirit-filled person from using any other gift
of the Spirit.

When the apostle Peter got directed by a vision from God
to go and preach to the house of Cornelius — a Gentile —
not a Jew like himself; he spoke these marvellous words of
comprehended truth:

> 34. *Then Peter opened his mouth, and said, Of*
> *a truth I perceive that God is no respecter of*
> *persons:*
> 35. *But in every nation he that feareth him, and*
> *worketh righteousness, is accepted with him.*
> — Acts 10:34–35

If you have never read Acts chapters 10 and 11 — please do
— it's a fascinating account of how Peter came to preach the
gospel to non-Jewish people — because God has poured out
His Spirit upon all flesh.

While we may not be in the habit of using all the gifts of the
Spirit — we can rest assured that if there is a need then God
will help us to use what we need.

It takes the exercising of our faith to operate these gifts and
as we pray about them and come to understand more about
them then we can all use those gifts as and when needed.

You could find that gifts like a *"word of wisdom"* or a *"word
of knowledge"* will get used by you when you witness to your
friends and family.

The Lord will bring to your remembrance words to say and
remind you of the content of the scriptures you have read
and for which you now know more about their meaning and
intent.

These verses from chapter 14 help us to see how we should

operate those more often used *"vocal"* spiritual gifts in the church:

> 23. *If therefore the whole church be come together*
> *into one place, and all speak with tongues,*
> *and there come in those that are unlearned, or*
> *unbelievers, will they not say that ye are mad?*
> 24. *But if all prophesy, and there come in*
> *one that believeth not, or one unlearned, he is*
> *convinced of all, he is judged of all:*
> 25. *And thus are the secrets of his heart made*
> *manifest; and so falling down on his face he will*
> *worship God, and report that God is in you of a*
> *truth.*
> 26. *How is it then, brethren? when ye come*
> *together, every one of you hath a psalm, hath a*
> *doctrine, hath a tongue, hath a revelation, hath*
> *an interpretation. Let all things be done unto*
> *edifying.*
> 27. *If any man speak in an unknown tongue, let*
> *it be by two, or at the most by three, and that by*
> *course; and let one interpret.*
> 28. *But if there be no interpreter, let him keep*
> *silence in the church; and let him speak to himself,*
> *and to God.*
> 29. *Let the prophets speak two or three, and let*
> *the other judge.*
> 30. *If any thing be revealed to another that sitteth*
> *by, let the first hold his peace.*
> 31. *For ye may all prophesy one by one, that all*
> *may learn, and all may be comforted.*
> 32. *And the spirits of the prophets are subject to*
> *the prophets.*
> 33. *For God is not the author of confusion, but of*
> *peace, as in all churches of the saints.*
> — 1 Corinthians 14:23–33

Everyone in God's church has the ability to speak with other tongues — we get warned in verse 23 that we must — **not** all speak in tongues at once.

Why?   Because any *"unlearned,"* or *"unbelieving"* visitor to the church meeting could conclude: *"You are mad."*

Look at verse 32 and 33: *"the spirits of the prophets are subject to the prophets"* — we do not lose our self control.

Of utmost importance: *"God is not the author of confusion."*

Look at verse 27 — *"let it be by two, or at the most by three, and that by course."*

The true church of God can and should operate these miraculous gifts of the Holy Spirit — tongues; interpretation of tongues; and prophecy — and their operation must get done decently and in order.

If your old church does not do that — find a new one that does know how to act in accordance with God's Word.

It's important for God to speak to us through the operation of those miraculous gifts.

The pastor or leader of the church meeting will invite the congregation to operate those Spiritual Gifts at an appropriate time.

We do not use the Spiritual Gifts at random times; we need to be singing praises to God or listening to the invited testimony from another brother or sister or paying attention to a Bible talk or remaining quiet to make it easier to hear announcements about important upcoming events.

There's always plenty of time for discussion and fellowship with other church members and visitors after the meetings conclude.

May The Lord bless you and keep you — to His soon return.

By the same author

Nonfiction

God redeems the reject
Recounts how the author, the reject, received the
precious gift from God that Jesus called — *"the
promise of the Father"* — 2025.
ISBN 9781764299725 (EPUB)
ISBN 9781764299732 (paper book)

Take a gawk
Another book on the Linux operating system —
this one concentrates on the AWK interpreter
— a programming system with extraordinary
capabilities — 2025.
ISBN 9781764299749 (EPUB)
ISBN 9781764299756 (paper book)

The Miracle Working God
Describes God's miracle working activity in the
previous 50 years of my life — 2025.
ISBN 9781764057868 (EPUB)
ISBN 9781764057875 (paper book)

Love, Joy, Peace
Living a better life by the Grace of God — 2025.
ISBN 9791764057844 (EPUB)
ISBN 9791764057851 (paper book)

Glory to God Everywhere You Are There
Describes the origins of my simple song of praise
from which I use its 3rd line as this title — 2025.
ISBN 9781764057820 (EPUB)
ISBN 9781764057837 (paper book)

Jesus Says You Must Be Born Again
The most important information this world
affords got given to us by Jesus Christ when He
used those five imperative words — 2025.
ISBN 9781764057813 (EPUB)
ISBN 9781764057806 (paper book)

Linux Clues
Tips and clues about using the Linux operating
system from a seasoned Linux user — 2025.
ISBN 9781764057882 (EPUB)
ISBN 9781764057899 (paper book)

9 dozen 9 character word puzzles
9 dozen 9 character word puzzles says it all;
over 100 puzzles to enjoy — 2025.
ISBN 9781764299701 (EPUB)
ISBN 9781764299718 (paper book)

Linux Bread Crumbs
Small morsels to help you learn to use the Linux
operating system — 2023.
ISBN 9798364005830 (paper book)

Paul's Question
Have you received the Holy Spirit? — 2023.
ISBN 9798857128381 (paper book)

To Day If You Will Hear His Voice
Encouragement to believe in God — 2022.
ISBN 9798831130669 (paper book)

Take Another Look
If you have come across the full gospel message of
Jesus Christ before and opted out — please take
another look — 2022.
ISBN 9798437605554 (paper book)

Song Lyrics
Notes and lyrics for 16 of my gospel songs with
some links to help you listen to those — 2022.
ISBN 9798434494120 (paper book)

Fiction

The Ravenscroft Algorithm
Fictitious cyber security crime — 2022.
ISBN 9798842106202 (paper book)

Broke Reef
Fictitious shipwreck on a West Australian Reef
set in the late 19th century — 2022.
ISBN 9798428316940 (paper book)